I Can Stand Up to Bullies

to Bullies

Finding Your Voice
When Others Pick on You

Written & Illustrated by Dagmar Geisler
Translated by Andrea Jones Berasaluce

Sky Pony Press
New York

Can I stand up to bullies?

I get angry sometimes. I get mad when plans don't work out. I become frustrated when I don't succeed at something. And I am embarrassed and sometimes disappointed in myself when I'm scared to try new things.

But what bothers me most is when I am bullied.

And what exactly are the differences?

An Argument...

...is about something.

Two people have different opinions or each one wants something different.

Maybe there was a misunderstanding.

Each person can give their opinion.

Through arguing, you can find a solution together. It may be sooner or it may be later when things calm down again.

Alright, then we'll take turns.

Today we'll do what you want and tomorrow what I want.

Bullying someone...

...is only to make fun of someone.

Someone who bullies isn't trying
to find a solution.

The person bullying just wants to anger the other person.

Or they just want the other person to feel bad.

A bully doesn't want to hear the other
person's response or opinion at all.

And if they do hear it,
their teasing will only get meaner.

Sometimes a bully will say:

You can't take a joke! We're just having fun!

Being picked on and teased is fun?
Is that even possible?

Yes, it's possible! Sometimes it's fun to tease or to play a few funny pranks on each other.

The best pranks cause *everyone* involved to laugh so hard they can't breathe.

But no one can *make* you find something funny. Not even if it was something you found funny in the past. You have the right at any point to say: "Stop! I don't like this anymore."

Or:

Things won't be less fun because of it. Quite the opposite!

When you're confident you're just having fun and know you can stop at any time, you're more likely to play along. In those cases, you can even dare to try a couple silly things you wouldn't normally agree to.

But no one has the right to tell you that you **must** have fun doing something.

But there are situations that don't feel like fun at all. Like when someone is in a bad mood and is mean to you because of it. That's not nice and, of course, is completely unfair. But it does happen.

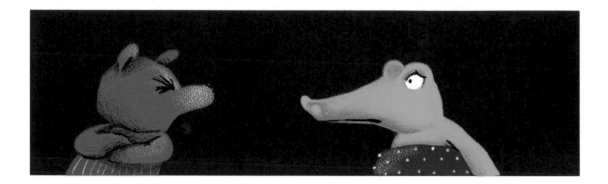

If you then apologize and maybe even share what happened to put you in such a bad mood, then others can better understand. And that helps you get along again.

But sometimes these situations can't be resolved
so easily. Instead, you become angry and hurt.
You don't know if it will ever stop.

It feels horrible when you're the kid that everyone
teases. No matter what you do, they always find a
reason to make of you. They laugh at you. They say
things about you that are none of their business or
that aren't true at all.

Maybe they also threaten to share embarrassing
stories about you if you don't do what they want.

Sometimes they go so far that you get the feeling that
the whole group hates you. Even the kids you thought
were your friends.

In this type of situation, sometimes it's very hard for the person doing the teasing to talk about why they're in such a bad mood. Or why they feel like hurting another kid's feelings by being mean to them.

Sometimes the bullies themselves don't even understand why they're being mean. Or they don't want anyone to figure out what's bothering them.

They may have also seen other people take out their frustrations on friends or family members. They might even think doing so is fine.

Instead of others noticing that I'm scared, I want them to be afraid of me.

I sometimes don't notice at all that the fun is over.

I tease because it's fun for me.

If I get angry, at least others notice I'm there.

No one likes me anyway, so I can get angry about that.

My uncle says that people from the next town over are all stupid. It's okay to make fun of them.

I've been getting bullied this whole time. Now I bully back.

But this isn't alright, because teasing and bullying hurt. These actions hurt the soul, and when your soul isn't doing well, you notice it in your body. For example, you may get a stomachache or headache. A kid who is constantly getting picked on or teased can lose their appetite, stop sleeping well, or become depressed.

That's the way it is.

Now you might think that this only affects kids who get teased and bullied. But what about the kids who witness it? What does that mean for them? And what should they do? Can they do anything at all?

When Lukas made fun of me again, I wished that someone would stand up for me. But no one said anything.
Lukas is my friend. I don't think what he did was good, but I'm on his side anyway.
I don't think what Lukas did was right, but it's not my friend that he teased.
I know. I wanted to say something but I didn't know what. And then it was too late.
I always tell myself that next time I'll say something, but then....
I'm afraid that then it'll all backfire on me.

Talking to others when something is bothering you is a good idea. It helps you mutually understand each other better. It helps to quickly stop teasing or to keep it from happening in the first place. It helps you have more fun, because things are better when people trust each other.

It sounds easy but it's often hard to get started. Especially if the bullying has been going on for a while. Getting help is a good idea. No one has to be alone in such a situation. And it's not tattling when you confide in someone and tell that person how you feel.

No one has to keep a terrible secret to themselves. A secret is bad when you don't feel comfortable with it.

By the way, you can practice this type of talking! It's best if you try it out together—always with the same group of people. It's important that everyone gets to speak and nobody is laughed at for their feelings. Each person shares with the others what they're feeling at that moment. But if you don't want to speak at that time, you don't have to.

Sometimes it seems like a bully is always the bully and a victim is always the victim. But that's not true. Anyone can be in either of those positions. Either way, it's helpful to recognize what's going on in any given situation.

IF I'M THE BULLY:

What is the reason for my teasing?

Did the kid that I picked on do something to me?
If that's the case, I should speak up.
Then we can talk it out and each person can state their opinion.

The other kid must have the right to defend themselves.
Just like I do.

However, the discussion can only be about something someone has done or said, not about who someone is. So these conversations can't be about how someone looks, where they're from or what their background is, or how they talk.

It's not okay to make fun of, threaten, or to go so far as to even hit someone. If any of these happen, I have to stop the argument. If I can't do it alone, I can confide in someone. If I do that, I have the right to be heard without being punished.

And I can apologize. Those who apologize for their behaviors and words are truly strong and brave.

IF I SEE OR HEAR SOMEONE BEING BULLIED:

Is it bullying? Or are they maybe arguing?

If it's bullying: How do I feel about it? Am I afraid to say something because then I'll get made fun of? Or do I secretly like what's going on?

Would I like to say something to help? Do I trust myself? Or do I not trust myself? Am I mad at myself if I don't trust myself? Am I perhaps scared?

I'm allowed to say: "I don't like what's happening. I don't think it's okay to pick on someone."

If I can't say anything in the moment, it will also help the kid later if I say: "I saw how you were teased. I don't think it's right." Then the kid will feel less alone.

Maybe we can get help together.

IF I'M SOMEONE WHO IS BULLIED:

Am I being teased or are we arguing? If it's an argument, I can state my side of it.

If I'm scared, I don't need to be ashamed. I can confide in someone and talk about my feelings.

Am I being attacked for who I am, like for my appearance or my origins? That's bullying.

If I'm afraid to state my views because I might be laughed at or picked on even more, it's bullying.

I can say that I don't think bullying is okay. If I feel like this will make things worse, I can get help.

I won't let anyone convince me that bringing it to someone's attention is tattling. Adults also get help if they are wronged. That's perfectly alright.

BULLYING

will ruin the fun.
We'd rather have fun.

Help & Guidance

USA

StopBullying.gov
U.S. Department of Health and Human
Services
200 Independence Avenue, S.W.
Washington, D.C. 20201
1-800-273-8255
www.stopbullying.gov

STOMP Out Bullying
220 East 57th Street
New York, NY 10022-2820
877- N0BULLY (877-602-8559)
info@stompoutbullying.org
www.stompoutbullying.org/helpchat

National Suicide Prevention Lifeline
1-800-273-TALK (8255)

GLBT National Youth Talkline
1-800-246-PRIDE (1-800-246-7743)

CANADA

Kids Help Phone (Canada)
300-439 University Ave
Toronto, ON M5G 1Y8
800-668-6868
Kidshelpphone.ca

Bullying Canada
471 Smythe Street
P.O. Box 27009
Fredericton, NB, E3B 9M1
877-352-4497
support@bullyingcanada.ca
www.Bullyingcanada.ca

Canada Suicide Prevention Service
1-833-456-4566

UK

Childline
NSPCC Weston House
42 Curtain Road
London EC2A 3NH
0800 1111
Childline.org.uk

Kidscape
2 Grosvenor Gardens
London SW1W 0DH
020 7823 5430
info@kidscape.org.uk

Samaritans
The Upper Mill
Kingston Road
Ewell, Surrey KT17 2AF
116 123
https://www.samaritans.org/
jo@samaritans.org

Afterword

So, what's the big deal with teasing?

I realized while creating this book that it's not an easy topic. It has as many different facets as there are people. And at some point, each of us will encounter it in one way or another.

In its harshest form, we call it "bullying" and hope that our children won't be affected by it. Whomever has experienced it even once knows what damage it can do.

I was once in such a situation during my school-age years. At that time, these things were not discussed. The word "bullying" wasn't even in our vocabulary. Nobody noticed how I withdrew more and more into myself. A characteristic of bullying is that victims often try to hide what's going on. A sense of shame arises within, and sometimes there's also the fear that the attacks will become more intense if you make known what's happening.

It was really bad for me back then. My grades dropped, and in the afternoons, I started burying myself in comic books. I have nothing against comics, but at the time, I even read ones I actually found abominable just to distract myself. When I had to repeat my classes, I was glad, as I could now steer clear of my aggressors. These experiences accompanied me for a long time, like a dark cloud. It wasn't until I started speaking to others about it that things got brighter for me.

I am glad that it is easier today to exchange ideas about such topics and also about one's feelings. This allows us to be aware of how others are doing. It's an important safeguard. And I hope that through my book I can encourage others to practice this over and over again.

A group in which a respectful discourse has become established is much more likely to avoid bullying situations. Once these groups are solid, such discourse allows for these situations to be cleared up quickly.

The best way to start this conversation is by asking: "How are you today?"

Dagmar Geisler

© Jahreiss.com

Dagmar Geisler has already supported several generations of parents in seeing their children through emotionally difficult situations. Through her "Safe Child, Happy Parent" picture book series, the author and illustrator sensitively deals with the most important issues related to growing up: from body awareness to exploring one's own emotional world to social interaction. There is always a dose of humor in her works—all the more so when things get serious.

Her books have been translated into twenty languages. She lives in Germany.

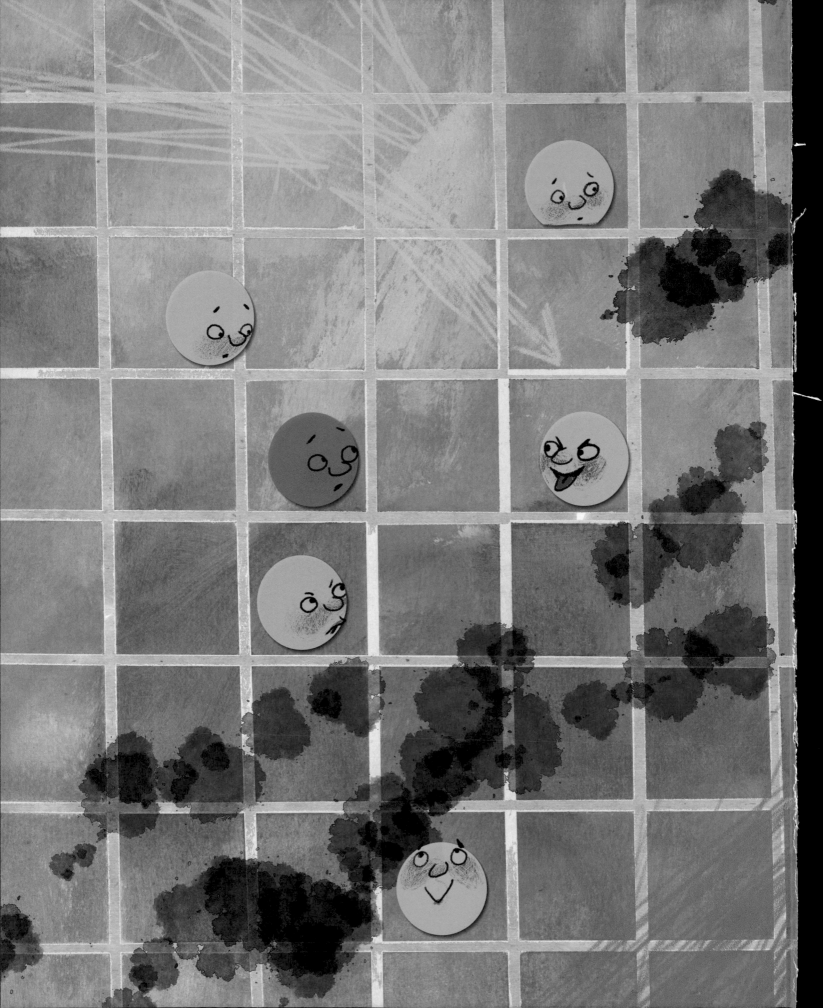